A Solution to
Homelessness in Yo

Valley View Senior Housing, Napa County,
California

Charles Durrett
with Jinglin Yang

A Solution to Homelessness in Your Town

Valley View Senior Housing, Napa County, California

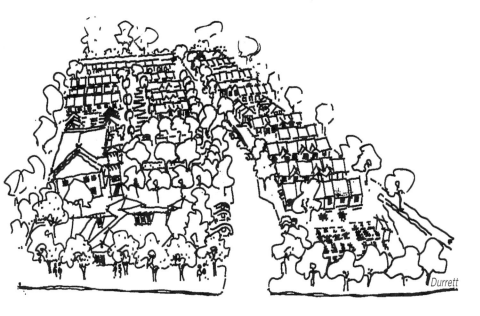

ORO Editions
Publishers of Architecture, Art, and Design
Gordon Goff: Publisher

www.oroeditions.com
info@oroeditions.com

Published by ORO Editions

Author: Charles Durrett
Photographer: Patrik Argast
Book Design: Jinglin Yang
Project Coordinator: Alejandro Guzman-Avila
Managing Editor: Jake Anderson

10 9 8 7 6 5 4 3 2 1 First Edition

ISBN: 978-1-935935-45-2

Color Separations and Printing: ORO Group Ltd.
Printed in China.

ORO Editions makes a continuous effort to minimize the overall carbon footprint of its publications. As part of this goal, ORO Editions, in association with Global ReLeaf, arranges to plant trees to replace those used in the manufacturing of the paper produced for its books. Global ReLeaf is an international campaign run by American Forests, one of the world's oldest nonprofit conservation organizations. Global ReLeaf is American Forests' education and action program that helps individuals, organizations, agencies, and corporations improve the local and global environment by planting and caring for trees.

This book is dedicated to all city, county, and state officials everywhere, and to their nonprofit housing partners, who, with vision and faith in their fellow citizens, set up the unhoused for long-term success by building communities and putting simple roofs over their heads. Which in turn creates real homes in true communities.

Contents

Introduction   **2**
The Location   **10**
The Site   **12**
Hill Town Village Inspiration   13
Homeless and Seniors   15
The New Birth   17
Abandoned Retaining Walls   25
Client-Approved Design   26
Why a Village?   27
Common House, Common Facilities   30
Clubhouse Interior   31
Exterior Spaces   33
The Grand Opening   35
The Look: A Vernacular Style   38
Floor Plans   40
Affordability   42
Services   45
Site Planning   49
Creativity   51
Funding   **54**
Accessibility   56
Safety and Security   59
Fire Suppression Systems in Fire Prone Areas   61
Sustainable Materials   63
Sustainable Construction   66
Renewable Energy   69

Contents

In Conclusion   **72**

Acknowledgments   **75**

Appendix:

    A - Affordable Villages Elsewhere   81

    B - Picturing the Homeless in California   82

    C - The FEMA Emergency Criteria   83

    D - Sample Resident Agreement   85

    E - Benefits of an Opportunity Village in Eugene, Oregon   88
        and to any Americans Experiencing People Without a
        Roof in Their Town.

    F - Faces of Change: Formally Homeless   89

About the Author   **93**

Afterword   **95**

Feasibility for New Sites   **96**

Bibliography   **97**

Part 1

Introduction

Close to one million people are unhoused in the United States today. Millions and millions are ill-housed—people living in shanties or leaky, moldy trailers. And millions more are mis-housed—in houses that are abusive in their loneliness, forlorn and empty at so many levels. We can do something about it. Actually, it's low-hanging fruit, should we choose to do something; impossible, if we do not. And it's essential, not only for the well-being of the individual, but also for the well-being of the State, and the society.

Current studies are overwhelmingly show that it is more cost effective, in terms of tax dollars earmarked for city, county, state, and federal governments, to house people than it is to just leave them outside. About $20k to $40k cheaper for each person per year. In the case of the unhoused, it also taxes our psyches and our emotions to see our neighbors sleeping on the sidewalk. It is difficult, if not impossible, to explain to our children and grandchildren how we Americans leave people outside in the cold—mentally challenged or not. Then, there is the moral issue.

There are too many camp sites, too few compact efficient, but comfortable and safe houses.

If you are motivated to get a new homeless housing project moving in your town, this book is the best place to start.

I wrote this book in 2020, right in the middle of the COVID-19 pandemic. An inordinate number of homeless people in this country are already extremely vulnerable. For them Covid-19 is horror atop of horror. After all, the homeless have no shelter in which to shelter-in-place.

Valley View Senior Housing is an affordable senior housing community built in 2019 in American Canyon, Napa County, California. Its housing consists of 70 units with an average of 500 ft^2.

If no one were to die from COVID-19 at Valley View Senior Housing because the members of this community discipline each other. And its residents are successfully sheltering-in-place—because they have a place.

On the day of this writing, 70 residents of a homeless shelter in San Francisco tested positive for COVID-19. On the same day Governor Gavin Newsom announced that, in total, 60,000 homeless in the state would have been ill-affected by the virus.

This book is for the about **2,900** city councilors of the **482** incorporated municipalities in California; to the about **2,900** city/town planning commissioners; to the **482** city/town managers; and to the **482** city/town community development directors; and to the **482** city/town planning directors; and the **58** California counties; and to their **290** Board of Supervisors; to the **290** county planning commissioners; to the **58** county chief administrators; **58** county mental health departments; to the **58** county sheriff's offices; and to the rest who want to make a difference, especially the approximate **200-plus** nonprofit housing developers in the State of California. We know that so many public servants wish to solve the homeless crisis but do not know the way forward. Here's a proven way.

Thousands and thousands of people want to solve this problem. They know the why, and now they can learn how. Starting with addressing that the challenges of homelessness is a nationwide issue. But for now, let's start with California. In fact, let's focus on the local level.

Franklin D. Roosevelt said that San Francisco people, for example, were as capable as anyone anywhere when they built the Golden Gate Bridge and the San Francisco–Oakland Bay Bridge in the midst of the Great Depression. Getting people from the outside will be a team sport. In every town, it takes only one person to get the ball rolling. This person takes a leadership role then, soon enough, others join and a senior housing community like Valley View Senior Housing (VVSH) is constructed. The logical point of departure to get one built in your town is this book, outlining this model project.

"Lombard Street"

After the first town meeting it was suggested that neighbors visit a similar project that we just finished in the town of Sonoma. The second meeting was much easier because it was obvious that it is possible to be sensitive to town-wide issues.

Part 2

The Location

Valley View is located at 1 Natalie Lane, in the city of American Canyon. The 3.5-acre parcel is zoned as a medium-density residential subdivision. The 56-foot hill on the property slopes from west to east and is surrounded by single-family homes, a sheep farm, and a firewood warehouse: a rural, semi-rural, and increasingly suburban context. Valley View is located close to Highway 29, which is the main artery for traffic running through the city. It is also less than five miles from Interstate 80, one of the main roadways used to travel throughout Northern California.

Part 3

The site with ruins of previous McMansion project.

The Site

The Valley View 3.5-acre site was bought by the City of American Canyon in Napa County, California, a brand-new town of about 21,000 residents located 35 miles northwest of San Francisco. Prior to the global economic recession of 2008, the site was owned by a developer that had begun construction of 17 large single-family houses. That project was eventually abandoned, and the site was purchased for $460,000 by the City. Once the property was obtained, city officials sent a request to nonprofit developers for proposals to build a 70-unit development for seniors with little or no means.

Twenty-nine organizations responded, of which 28 proposals were received, all essentially the same: a single, three- or four-story building that would be built over a concrete podium with underground parking, or a big box surrounded by parking with a double-loaded corridor inside. Because of the nature of the site, including a dramatic 56-foot slope from west to east, the single-box appeared like the most evident and cost-effective option.

The infamous retaining walls.

Hill Town Village Inspiration

A significant challenge was to create what some have referred to as a "hill town" solution; abandoning the one-building form, we adopted the hill town possibility. The design was to take on the characteristics of small hillside villages that you might see perched on hilly terrain in Southern Europe. MDA set out to create a village instead of a project. Among the goals was to get residents exercising, connecting, and interacting with each other in a way that would foster community and mutual support.

Although more typical and even sometimes more appropriate, the point is to understand what is appropriate in each case via the thorough feasibility phase which is different than the design phase. A box in a pool of asphalt is not always so. Since when did "setback" become a good word. These environments are quite the opposite of conducive to pedestrians.

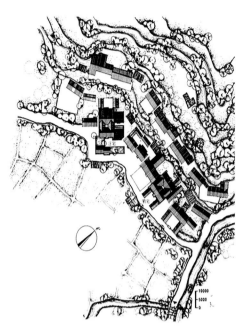

Ancient Chinese village concept photo. Flows along topo lines marrying the people, the land, and in this case, the farm. It emphasizes the continuation of place-making. That does not turn its back on history: human-scale, compact, and intimate.

This drawing captures the essence of this project. Where environments bring the VVSH people together. A centripetal environment with small courtyards and gardens.

Homeless and Seniors

Two other requirements for this project had everything to do with the residents themselves. First, it had to be designed with the needs of seniors in mind: one resident per household is to be at least 55 years old to qualify. Secondly, the residents needed to identify as one of the following:

- United States military veteran who was homeless
- A homeless person
- A person who was previously homeless
- A person who was at high risk of becoming homeless

Satellite Affordable Housing Associates (SAHA) and the architects needed to take these requirements into account from the outset. As advocates for the homeless in our own hometowns, we felt a responsibility to create something that other city governments would find useful to duplicate. That meant that the Valley View project had to be affordable, beautiful, and highly functional for this population. The City wanted it to sit pretty in the landscape, and it also needed a return on its investment. If the project stalled into insolvency, we knew that other towns and cities would be hesitant to invest in larger-scale projects that aid low-income or homeless people.

10'-0" MIN.

The New Birth

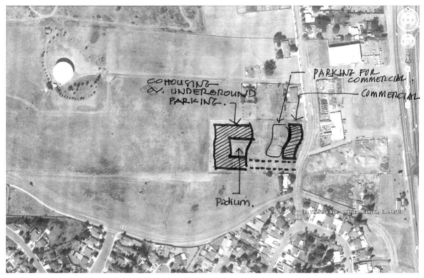

First sketch, like everyone else's.

On a Saturday, just weeks before the proposals were due, I traveled to the site to find inspiration. When I left my studio in Nevada City, California (two hours away), I had resigned myself to the idea that a single building was the only option for this site. At that point, I was going there simply to seek inspiration on how to decorate the big box. And I was feeling pretty dispirited that all I was doing was searching for the best of the contemporary architectural styles to virtually warehouse people.

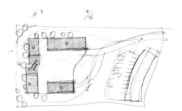

Second sketch, starting to pull apart.

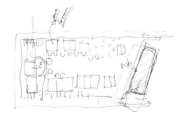

Third sketch, mitosis beguns in earnest.

When I arrived, I climbed to the highest northwest corner of the site and just sat there to wonder about other possibilities. I first considered the lives of the people who would be living there, and the fact that each of them had faced significant adversity. I also thought about the role that community needed to play in their lives going forward, and whether that could be created with the current single-building, big-box design. I began sketching and measuring, and when I left the site that evening, a new design began to emerge that broke with the 28 other proposals. Instead of one building it would be 24.

I knew that a multistory, one-building, double-loaded corridor solution didn't feel right at all; it would be more or less "hoteling" people. Outside of an urban context, a single large building doesn't make sense for housing. Put another way, one big building in a rural setting would feel a little bit like people storage.

One building solution. The best solution these days is rarely the obvious one.

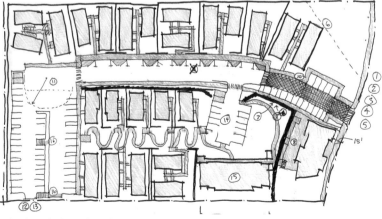

Early feasibility sketch.

Instead of a single building, I conceived a design of 1-bedroom homes, also with a two-story building with four 2-bedroom units (the second bedroom for a possible live-in caregiver), a solar-covered parking area, and a clubhouse structure that could be used by anyone in the community. The original concept proposed by the other organizations of one large building instead became 24 buildings and 58 cottages, each with a front porch to sit and watch the world go by, and a back porch for outdoor privacy. Direct access between private dwellings and semi-private front porches increased the use of outdoor space.

Front porches are spaces between houses and the community—a place where people can be a part of the common area, yet also be semi-private. They provide a "soft edge" where people flow easily between indoors and outdoors many times a day, and where they are able to readily pop out and say hello. The Valley View design encourages this by avoiding impediments between indoor and outdoor spaces.

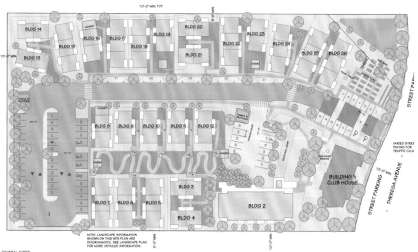

But a way was needed to connect the houses, and that solution was not obvious on this relatively small site with a steep hill. While sitting on the hill that day, bemused by the passing clouds above, one of San Francisco's popular attractions came to mind: the famous crooked street of San Francisco. The 1000 block of Lombard Street snakes its way down an extreme slope, along with the switchbacks created by this design. Though untraditional, the functionality of the street made sense, and it inspired the "Lombard Street solution" for Valley View. I drew repeating S-turns into part of the design and used it to connect houses in the heart of the site's slope. I walked the dozen curves as I left the site with the waning light. The result promotes interaction between neighbors and encourages activity and exercise. It wasn't an obvious solution, but it worked. The vegetable gardens, the bocce ball court, and "Lombard Street," all would help keep the seniors active and connected.

Another important source of inspiration was the background of the residents themselves. Many are veterans. I couldn't stop thinking about the inadequate support and resources that so many servicemen and servicewomen received when they return home. Also, too many men and women don't come home at all. Considering this, the idea of the "three soldiers" began. The clubhouse includes three standing dormers that represent three soldiers standing at attention in formation.

Housing the vets: 3 soldiers in formation at attention, one fallen comrade on the left.

It also has one lowered vent dormer, which represents a fallen comrade. These designs were very small ways of acknowledging and paying tribute to the service of the residents.

Early Sketch.

Abandoned Retaining Walls

Original ziggurat.

Left over from the original development, abandoned in 2008, were 26 five- to six-foot-high retaining walls scattered throughout the site. Every other developer that submitted a proposal to the city recommended tearing them out completely, which would have cost the project over a million dollars. We were determined to use them, and eventually I found a structural engineer (Murphy Burr Curry, San Francisco) who would certify them. Too often we just tear down whatever is there to get a blank canvas, and in this case, that would have been too expensive. It would have also eviscerated the character of the terraced hill town. The problem of the existing retaining walls turned out to be an advantage—constraints turned into opportunity. Easy building sites are hard to come by these days. Creativity has to be a big part of every solution. Leaving the existing retaining walls was the key.

Kept the existing retaining walls.

Client-Approved Design

Brent Cooper, head of Community Development in American Canyon, said that the designs by MDA provided a clear path toward the creation of a community and fit what the town wanted. The City of American Canyon had two visions to choose from: a strip commercial big box, or a village. They chose to go the way of the village. We understand that the bigger box is sometimes less costly and more appropriate. In this case it was neither.

Why a Village?

When buildings are clustered together, they create walkable streets—and streets lead to close and useful destinations. Streets and buildings create outdoor rooms. A walkable street is where village life manifests, and this is what makes a village a village. The streets are fronted by porches, balconies, flowers, front doors, and kitchen windows, rather than garage doors, driveways, car parking, and hedges. In Valley View's case, fronts of houses have soft edges, private backyards, and clear hierarchy. To create the richness of a hilltop community, such as what exists in Southern France, made the most sense. These communities have a distinctive style, and they feature vibrant local materials.

Sonoma Affordable Housing Project

Early sketch

People relate to each other most healthfully at the horizontal level. The village setting accomplishes eye-to-eye relationships. This setting not only creates safer streets, but also encourages people to walk and encourages people to talk. Cars are very much de-emphasized. The walkways become social places and a children's playground for visiting grandchildren. One can sit at his or her front porch, chat with the neighbors going by, all while watching the visiting grandkids play. One can also knock on his or her neighbor's window to ask for a cup of flour without driving anywhere. The sense of place emerges when there is life between the buildings. There is no reason not to make housing feel like an ensemble, a collection, a village, instead of a disparate suburb, a campus, or an institution. And since the buildings are relatively small in this village concept—and most villages grow one small building at a time—it can still feel organic, even natural. It gives the sensation of being close together, more intimate, more knowing, but not claustrophobic. It's a design that respects and enhances both community life and personal privacy.

A proud resident.

A village has texture, varied colors, interest, detailed nuance, and very few missing teeth—no blank walls, no vignette devoid of interest. It has places along the way to sit, to just be, and to commune. A village feels like a village.

A livable village doesn't just happen by accident in the 21st century. We seem to have lost our ability as a social species to create villages one building at a time, naturally and organically, generation by generation. Today, creating a village is a conscious and deliberate act.

Free range grandchildren. Now a grandma can be grandma compared to their more compromised environments previously.

Common House, Common Facilities

The common house is located in the southeastern corner of the property and sits adjacent to the only two-story building, which contains four 2-bedroom units. The common terrace is right outside the common house. The common terrace is a place for the residents to have occasional common meals together outside and a place for the residents to socialize. The adjoining outdoor games court offers views of the community and garden area, making it a natural gathering place.

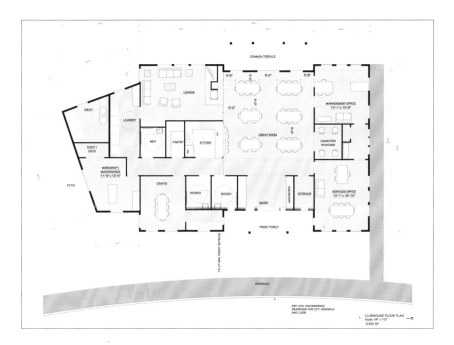

Clubhouse Interior

The interior of the common house/clubhouse is warm and inviting, and features a two-sided fireplace. The clubhouse has a common kitchen, from which the cooks can see all comings and goings – and a common dining area. Every house has its own kitchen, of course, but the clubhouse affords the opportunity for residents to break bread together—which is probably the most timeless means of sustaining community.

When the public health nurse comes to give immunization shots, a separate place is needed. A place is also needed for mental health support, social security counseling, and more. This facility, the clubhouse, uplifts the entire community by making it easy to provide what is otherwise a never-ending and encumbering logistics labyrinth.

The common space takes pressure off the small cottages, especially for couples.

A Veterans Health Administration (VHA) office and other management offices are also located in the clubhouse. These necessary offices do not feel bureaucratic. They are designed to be supportive spaces for the residents. This helps the professionals who work there to feel that their work is important and respected.

And of course the clubhouse is home to one of the three laundry facilities.

The common house/clubhouse is a necessary extension of the small private houses. The clubhouse is essential to making sure people don't get isolated and lonely, which is a death knell for about 40 percent of seniors, according to the *Psychology Today* magazine.

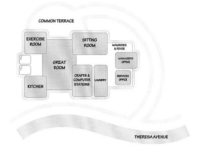

Early bubble diagram

Exterior Spaces

Besides common exterior socializing spaces, the front and back porches of each private house provides residents with their own exterior, secluded space and a semi-private front porch.

A sense of entry, a sense of home.

Something happens when you know your neighbor. You don't mind them approaching you as you read the paper on the front porch—in fact, you might anticipate it. Two or three seniors playing Scrabble together on a front porch is infinitely more interesting than two or three seniors watching television alone in their own house. Back porches are saved for more private occasions, and here privacy is well respected. I've noticed that at Valley View, residents often talk to each other when one resident is on their front porch. They might be talking about the issues of the day, like the new covey of quail that has just moved on site, or

"I'm going to work in the garden this afternoon—interested?" or, "Hey, I'm going to the store later today—do you want a lift", or "Do you need me to pick you up anything?" Neighbors giving each other rides, for example, saving individuals and the county considerable money. A functioning community of people who know each other, care about each other, and support each other can save government on average $30,000 per person, per year compared to those same individuals being solely dependent upon county services.

The Grand Opening

The residents of Valley View, besides being appreciative, appeared a bit shell-shocked when they moved in in the spring of 2019. Sleeping outside will do that.

During the grand opening, one of the residents, Matt, gave a speech. Where he started with the question, "You know that freeway you guys drove in on? I was under that freeway for more than six years, and I'm a Vietnam veteran, and now I have a home." Later, he said, "When I came to see my new home for the first time, I thought that I had gone to heaven. And I said to myself, I will be staying here until I actually do go to heaven."

MDA and others took up a collection of household wares in the larger community and delivered a couple of pickup loads. Many of these new residents were starting from nothing but a wet sleeping bag.

The same off-site neighbors who resisted the building of these new homes early on now come with supplies for their new neighbors.

Tables were set up in the clubhouse and were covered with kitchenware, blankets, toilet paper, and other household items. The residents rotated in. For me, the most impressive thing was a resident who carefully picked out a salt and a pepper shaker. She also picked out a box load of other kitchenware but not as carefully. She carried a salt and a

pepper shaker to her new small cottage, and I carried her box. She walked them home and then put them deliberately in the middle of her new card/dining table. Then she said, "There, I'm home. I have a home." Then she started to cry. The salt and pepper shakers, for her, was a key symbol for "I'm home now. I have a home now."

The grand opening day. Neighbors, city of officials, everyone is proud.

The Look: A Vernacular Style

The town of American Canyon is a traditional horse and cattle rural setting in the northern San Francisco Bay Area, with a sheep farm still next door. We took inspiration from the agrarian-style architecture, sometimes referred to as homestead architecture, that exists there. It is a simple and elegant enough but with some detail. In particular, such details include corner trim, which makes each structure easier and less costly to build, and easier to maintain.

Next door neighbors

Homestead architecture

In San Francisco tradition, color is used to mitigate the all-too-frequent cloudy gray skies. This distinctive and even vibrant look is waning in American Canyon, slowly being eclipsed by a more nondescript, "everywhere" suburban look. Valley View was our attempt to resurrect, if not bolster, that more textured historic feel, but with a very contemporary ode to energy efficiency (window canopies), accessibility, and clearly not suburban—but clearly a neighborhood.

Salvaged materials saved some costs, and just as important, added character. The tile surrounding the fireplace in the clubhouse used to be the roofing tile that the architects salvaged some years prior.

Floor Plans

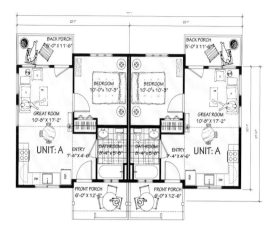

Duplex cottages

The more types of house plans there are and the more expressive each individual house is, the more every square foot of construction costs. Therefore, MDA restricted the floor plans to only three basic designs:

- Fifty-eight 1-bedroom cottage-like units (450 ft², 42 m²)
- Eight 1-bedroom stacked flat units (560 ft², 52 m²)
- Four 2-bedroom units (typical unit size is 875 ft², 83 m²). For the older population, two bedrooms were necessary in case they need to host a temporary caregiver.

By using the exact same floor plans for each 1-bedroom unit, the development saved considerable money. The savings on the private houses also allowed more essential common facilities necessary to assist these good people.

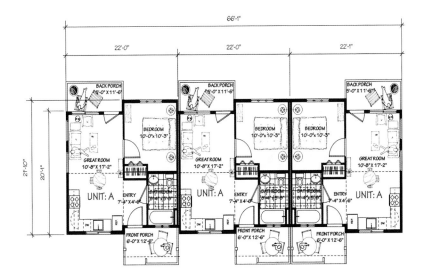

Triplex cottages

Bottom floor of two-story building. Second floor is the same.

Affordability

Since the late 1980s, MDA has designed more than 50 cohousing communities, and cost control was absolutely essential to every one of them.

The main requirement of the Valley View clients, the City of American Canyon and the nonprofit Satellite Affordable Housing Associates (SAHA), was affordability. All the prospective residents sat at the bottom of the Social Security income spectrum, and now many of them could finally receive Social Security benefits because they would have an address. American Canyon is not a wealthy town, and it is subject to careful oversight from every angle. And SAHA was also stringently accountable. Every dollar spent needed to be accounted for and needed to add value.

The MDA architects, SAHA, and Midstate Construction met numerous times during the preconstruction phase.

Unfortunately, one costly item that we had to remove from the plans to keep it affordable, was the elevator (which saved $100,000), but which reduced the roll-in (accessible to wheel chairs) units, by six. However, 64 units with roll-in access remained. It took several meetings to fit the project into budget. Meanwhile, in the super-heated construction market in the San Francisco Bay area, construction costs could not have been more compounded.

If a one-building, multi-level solution had been applied in this case, it would have very likely become too expensive to complete. One-story buildings (cottages) are simply cheaper to build—the one-building concept is simpler at the site plan level only. For example, Valley View Senior Housing had 21 framers

on the 39,000-square-foot project. From what I witnessed, only a couple of them had much prior experience. It is possible to build one-story cottages this way—that is, with less skilled labor. Between the extra million dollars it would have taken to remove the existing retaining walls, the two million dollars or more to build the podium, and more skilled labor, this project, like too many others in this era, might not have been built at all.

This is not to suggest that multi-story buildings are inappropriate elsewhere. MDA had completed a five-story building for formerly homeless people in San Francisco, a 5-story affordable project in Oakland, and lots of multistory buildings, including an 11-story building in Tokyo. However, at the American Canyon site, that decision would have been preclusive, and the one-story solution was applied. Making this studied decision was founded on the all-important feasibility study.

Services

As a housing provider for nearly two decades, SAHA has seen the tremendous impact that their service programs have made in the lives of their residents, especially for seniors whose health and welfare is greatly improved by staying engaged in an active and supportive community. SAHA is committed to providing the following programs to their senior residents at Valley View Senior Homes:

- Computer training. Tutorials in using email, Skype, and browsing the web are offered in the shared computer lab.
- Counseling seniors who were veterans and had been homeless for an extended period of time.
- Counseling for others who had been homeless or just need help.
- Health management and preventative screening and testing for conditions such as diabetes and high blood pressure. Nutritional workshops are also being provided to the residents, as well as assistance with enrolling in MediCal/Medicare and staying current on program changes.
- Support resident safety during the COVID-19 outbreak. It is infinitely easier in this setting, where people are being better educated about the risks and the hygienics than where they had been previously.

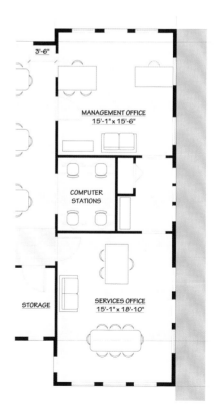

- Exercise classes and walking group opportunities. Management encourages peer-led exercise opportunities, such as walking groups, tai chi, and strength training. SAHA brings fitness professionals on site for specialty classes such as yoga and line dancing for spinal health.
- Gardening club. SAHA contributes funds annually to the on-site gardening club to pay for mulch, fertilizer, seeds/seedlings, and tools.

- Disaster preparedness. SAHA sponsors American Red Cross trainings at the site to educate and encourage residents to develop personal preparedness plans. Emergency plans and evacuation procedures are posted in common areas and reviewed annually with residents.
- Weekly events. SAHA hosts social events such as movie nights, coffee hour, and weekly potlucks that are consistent with the current needs and interests of residents.

In addition, the Veterans Health Administration (VHA) provides medical treatment, substance abuse and mental health counseling, and on-site case management for the householder who is a veteran.

What SAHA is best known for are the affordable neighborhoods they create. Of equal importance is the management of its developments. SAHA knows, like all nonprofit housing developers, that for them to

be eligible for succeeding projects, the buildings need to be appropriate and the residents have to be better-than-average neighbors.

There are 3 laundry facilities on site like this white one on the right with 2 washers, 2 dryers and clothes lines.

Sitting room in the clubhouse.

The temple to recycling. Reuse, Repair, Recycle, Rejoice.

Site Planning

The Valley View Senior Housing site plan is walkable and rollable, with the clubhouse design, a comfortable common outlet that makes the small houses comfortable. The cottages have the kitchen at the front of the house so that you might wave to those who walk by. It is designed to give the residents a sense of community and a sense of belonging, as well as privacy.

Personalized front porch

Warmth, why not?

Car-free walkable villages, that's where people connect. It's an old world pattern of human habilation on its way back.

As stated in *Creating Cohousing: Building Sustainable Communities* by Kathryn McCamant and Charles Durrett:

As dramatic demographic and economic changes continue to shape our society, many of us feel the effects of isolation in our personal lives. Many people feel alone, isolated, and disconnected: whether unhoused or mishoused, this is particularly trying. Individuals want the elements of traditional neighborhoods—family, community, a sense of belonging, respect that are so sorely missing in our society. This cluster housing concept reestablishes many of the advantages of traditional villages within the context of a 21st century life.

Creativity

All buildings have sagas, complex and circuitous stories, involving meetings with the neighbors, city officials, city hearings, and vendors for windows, carpeting, and roofing to best assure that you are getting the best value possible.

One of the small slices of the Valley View story is about the slate tile for the fireplace in the clubhouse. The slate roofing was removed from a horse stable built in 1900 by two Swedish brothers to house the horses for the then East Bay trolley at 3427 Alcatraz Avenue in what's now downtown Berkeley, California. Later, the slate was covered with an inch of tar. When MDA was remodeling the stable into a mixed-use building, we discovered the old roofing. During a cold, rainy winter, we removed the slate from that steep roof, one piece at a time, probably saving just about 10 percent of it. After cleaning and trimming it, we realized just how beautiful it could be.

The roofing slate is the hearth and facing at the fireplace.

Living room in a cottage

Kitchen in a cottage

Common house ceiling above

Bedroom in a cottage

Part 4

Funding

Every nonprofit housing developer receives their funding from a variety of sources. On average, about seven funders are usually involved. The Valley View project however received funding from 16 funders, including the State of California, Napa County, the City of American Canyon, Wells Fargo Bank, and a dozen other private companies, such as Home Depot. The larger number of funding sources was needed because this project faced many challenges and demands, such as providing accessibility to almost each household located on a steep slope. The many donors, small to large, of SAHA cannot be included in their entirety here but know that much appreciation is due and attention was paid to the responsibility of wise use of funding.

Groundbreaking day

The aftermath of the 2008 economic crash provided its own set of challenges. Simply stated, too few qualified subcontractors were still in business. And all construction materials rose in price: the cost of framing, concrete, roofing, and siding were simply rising.

The rash of large and destructive California fires also raised construction costs considerably.

But the issues of funding and construction costs were not on anyone's mind at the groundbreaking ceremony. All 16 funders came to celebrate.

I had never seen that before, even for a previous project that had only seven funders. A party-like atmosphere permeated this milestone event. After years and years of talking about the tragedy of homelessness in the region, especially in regard to veterans, these funders were giddy with the feeling that finally they got to be a part of the solution, and they were very proud.

The two-story building

Accessibility

An important criteria at Valley View was handicap accessibility. Many of the residents have mobility issues. All the requirements of the Americans with Disabilities Act had to be complied with, all while on a site with a 56-foot drop. As mentioned, 64 of the units would be roll-in. All the units' bathrooms and kitchens were adaptable. The houses were woven together in a way that meant that high-functioning sidewalks were critical.

The desire for community, visitability, and accessibility led to creating places to sit and discuss the issues of the day, watch grandchildren, tend the vegetable garden, or I just need to talk to somebody. In other words, like so many other aspects of this design (such as sustainability), accessibility is hugely facilitated by community. In real terms, cooperation and giving a damn about each other trumps architecture. But appropriate architecture makes that possible.

Moving in

"Lombard Street"

Amenities that would encourage activity and exercise were integrated into the design. These included outdoor terraces, balconies, courtyards, lawn space, a bocce ball court, the all-important front porch, and space for a small community garden. Since this site was being used as a healthy senior living community, the design needed to support and to inspire movement.

The final design requirement set forth by the City was practicality. It needed to be high functioning and promote independence as much as possible. A single-building design would have simplified all the processes, but it would have come at the cost of a sense of a neighborly community. No one wants to stand in a hotel corridor when it's gorgeous California weather outside. Other than emergencies, conventions and vacations, the literature strongly suggests the need for seniors to readily relate to the outdoors if at all possible.

Moving in

Neighbors talking. An important indicator of a successful project.

An important point of the project was to create physical conditions that encourage these residents, through interaction with others, to gain abilities and grow more capable every day, at every level.

Houses that relate to each other also lead people to relate with each other, which ultimately evolves into a village. This encourages people to know each other, to care about each other, and to support each other at some basic level. If it doesn't work socially, why bother? The preliminary sketch on page 14 is the genesis to the solution.

Safety and Security

People relating to each other, people helping each other: this is not rhetoric. This is how you keep people safe and promote emotional security. Few Valley View residents have vehicles. If they can, those who own cars give others rides to places, such as the doctor, relieving government entities of costly and inefficient elderly transportation programs. Offering rides also helps people who no longer feel comfortable driving. It is understood that the county would step up when needed; however, we have found that the immediate community itself, working in its own best interest, actually serves itself well.

Donations so that people can set the house up.

Too often many precious resources are left on the table in affordable housing. Valley View's primary asset for success has to be the residents themselves, and their motivations: They can save money in the long-term, they can help each other, and some can participate with management. In another affordable senior housing project, we utilized considerable community-building techniques. For example, we put on participation workshops where residents help landscape, clean, and even do some light maintenance. That approach paid off in huge dividends in helping to reduce the cost of management and in building camaraderie.

"We need communities that deliberately foster close social bonds. There are growing housing movements in which residents share chores and tend to common spaces together... There are about 150 cohousing communities in the U.S., but more are being built."

– Susan Pinker in Disconnection, published in Psychology Today, April 2018

A healthy community has to be the first priority.

Fire Suppression Systems in Fire Prone Areas

In California these days, every fire-related precaution must be taken:

- Fire resisting envelopes; nonflammable siding and roofing
- Fully sprinkled, even at one-story cottages
- Fire extinguisher every 75 feet outside; fire extinguishers for every interior
- No smoking on site
- Fire hydrants every 200 feet

...even volunteer fire suppression if necessary.

Volunteers at a 34-unit multi-family complex in the Sierras.

Ultimately, community is the key to fire safety. There is no substitute for community residents looking out for each other. It works. Fire safety is enhanced, and police are called much less frequently and fewer false alarms, saving the town money. It is well documented that a sense of community (folks who know each other) leads to a sense of healthy identity, which leads to far less aberrant behavior. Most important, each resident takes on a sense of accountability and responsibility for their behavior.

Sustainable Materials

Do construction materials matter? Absolutely. Which ones are inexpensive? Sustainable? Low-maintenance? Look good?

People take care of what they love, and people love what is beautiful. That said, the materials for each project are different and appropriate for that project.

LANDSCAPING

Native Plantings

- Low-water plants that are native to the area
- Xeriscaping
- Integrating edible plants that can easily grow in the area

PERMEABLE PAVERS

Calstone

- Permeable for storm water mitigation
- Regional production to minimize transportation distance within 500 miles
- Color and shape variety
- Smooth surface for ADA compliance
- Meets load requirements for fire truck access

www.calstone.com

GLASS EXTERIOR ENTRY DOORS

Simpson Performance Series

- Wood construction (Wood sources from sustainably managed forests) with Ultrablock Technology provides increased durability against weather
- Insulated glass to let sunlight in and keep heat out
- Certified lowest possible emissions of formaldehyde in wood based products for VOCs

www.simpsondoor.com

SIDING

James Hardie HardiePlank

- Increased durability as compared with wood siding with less maintenance
- Matches wood siding aesthetic
- Primed for optimum color acceptance

www.jameshardie.com

RECYCLED PAINT

Visions Recycling Products

- Recycled unused architectural paint
- Paints are high quality, recycled content, latex paint products and are available in many colors
- Used as undercoat

www.kellymoore.com

RADIANT BARRIER

Polar-Ply Radiant Barrier

- Integral with plywood roof sheathing for new construction (no additional labor)
- Reduces summer cooling loads - blocks 97% of summer radiant heat
- Flame retardant adhesive used to bind reflective membrane to plywood

www.polar-ply.com

CLASS A ASPHALT SHINGLE ROOFING

GAF Roofing (Timberline Cool Series)

- Warranty protection for the first 10 years
- Uses minimal natural resources
- The Cool Series reflects sunlight to help reduce attic heat build up and save energy

www.gaf.com

OUTDOOR BENCHES

Windsor Teak Furniture

- Teak construction (wood sourced from sustainably managed forests)
- Construction durability suited to commercial conditions

www.windsorteakfurniture.com

PLANTER BEDS

Gronomics

- Eliminates bending over and back issues
- 100% Western Red Cedar and constructed in the USA
- Comes finished or unfinished
- Size options: 34x48x32, 24x48x30, or 18x34x32

www.gronomics.com

Sustainable Construction

The main point of this book is to get people housed, and housed in a community setting. This is critical. But other factors reside on top of that moral plateau as well. Challenges such as climate change, accessibility, low maintenance, sustainability, and being ready for the next pandemic and more.

Valley View Senior Housing project is certified as GreenPoint Rated "Platinum." GreenPoint Rated is the most trusted home rating system in California. It provides proof that the home has been built to high environmental standards. All topics are taken into consideration, including energy efficiency, water conservation, indoor air quality, resource conservation, and livable communities.

Incessant construction overnight to keep on budget, on schedule, and no leaks.

1

Super efficient, blown-in insulation in the walls and roofs help maintain cool temperatures indoors during summer, and traps heat indoors and keeps the chilly temperatures outdoors during winter. Insulation helps the building work like a thermos.

2

Extra thick and dense sheetrock in the walls and ceilings, and light weight concrete floor toppings help maintain a consistent temperature. It slows the transfer of summer outdoor heat and keeps your home cooler. During winter, it slows the transfer of winter indoor heat and keeps your home warm.

3

Radiant barriers installed in the roof reflect heat from the sun, and prevent heat from entering the building during summer months. Also maintains warm indoor temperatures during winter by blocking heat from escaping.

4

Solar panels on the roof collect heat from the sun and deliver it to the houses.

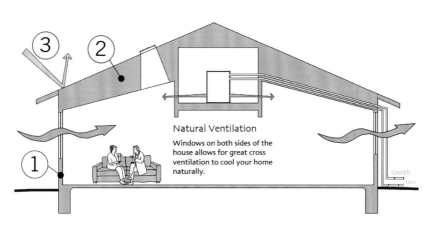

Natural Ventilation

Windows on both sides of the house allows for great cross ventilation to cool your home naturally.

Coolth
Heat

5

The low winter sun penetrates deep into your home through high windows. Overhangs outside protect the homes from summer sun and heat gain.

6

Ceiling fans can help keep you cool during hot days, but use them only while you are in the room, as they will cool the body but actually heat the room.

7

Low-e windows for their higher insulation value.

8

During cool nights in the summer, you can remove more hot air by turning on your bathroom exhaust fan. Open a window to allow cool air to replace the hot air you are getting rid of.

9

People can share resources. Households have equal access to the common facilities like the lounge area, dining room, craft room, computer lab, full facility kitchen.

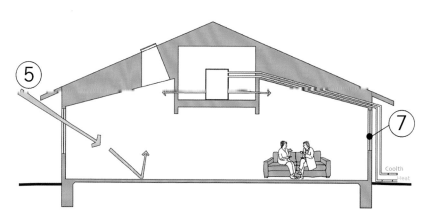

Renewable Energy

We installed a 50 kilowatt solar-covered parking area as well as extra insulation, allowing the sunlight in on sunny winter days and keeping it out on hot summer days. There is solar mass in the houses and all means of economical design to keep the energy bills low. That is why we achieved the "Platinum" rating. But, again, it's cooperation among the residents and managements that pays the highest dividends.

Residents.

Part 5

Feels like a village.

In Conclusion

So someone needs to get it started out, who in turn will compel others to join the sentiment and direction. Then a solution arises, as it did in American Canyon. It will be the thing to do.

Things will shift along the way. And while it doesn't seem that the what should matter, just get a roof over their heads. But that's not true. We can do the appropriate what. When a village is called for, we do that. When a single building is called for, we do that. But as much community as possible is always called for. People helping each other is just as real as the government doing some heavy lifting. In some cases, it's a great deal of volunteer work. In other cases, it's the government and the private non-profits that play a bigger role. But I've been in too many countries who can manage without homelessness, and so can we. When I asked in Denmark "Why do I see no homeless here?" Their response was, "Because if I see someone sleeping outside, I say to myself, 'That could be my brother.'"

Feels like a home.

And too often someone in the U.S. has said to me, "Chuck, it's Darwinian." Those two sentiments are exactly opposite sentiments. We have as much money as they do, and plenty of land. Let's do something – because we know we can.

I just spoke to a homeless woman who "lives" in the door front of the shop downstairs. Everyone, especially her, would be so much better off if she had neighbors, structure, purpose, and a reason to live. I feel that this is what they mean by "Darwinian".

There is too much humanity left on the table. We find over and over again, if we can get these humans into supportive communities, they can better reach their potential, and so can society.

Warm and cozy attached cottages.

Detail brings delight.

Maybe she'll just go away. That's not how the leaders of American Canyon felt when they decided to make shelter – and successfully did so.

The Valley View project has proven that the time is now. Many people are just plain tired of the incapacity to approach the multi-layered challenges of homelessness, affordable housing, and the valley and peak of community decay and community development. How can it not be obvious that housing solutions are being found and applied in some areas – solutions that meet unique community conditions.

Getting a roof over peoples' heads is the evident first approach for housing the homeless. But our approach is community first. Set the community up for success and create a world where it is easier to support each other. This means tapping into the strengths of the residents – not just policing them. Everyone is always surprised how much people can do for each other and for themselves when managed properly. Not only does it save the government considerable money, it also makes living there more enjoyable for everyone around.

Acknowledgments

This book would not have been possible without everybody who got involved: to all who were drawn to make this project happen and to those drawn to help tell this story.

We want to thank the residents of Valley View who shared their heartfelt sentiments.

The City of American Canyon: Brent Cooper, head of Community Development.

The developer: Satellite Affordable Housing Associates (SAHA); Susan Friedland, executive director; Eve Stewart, director of Development; Aubra Levin, project manager #1; Carrie Lutjens, project manager #2.

The architects: McCamant & Durrett Architects; we have said a lot about us so far, but in particular Gary Burke, Architect. Thank you to all the architects and designers/implementers from the McCamant & Durrett Architects' staff for manifesting the dream.

Left to right: Visiting CEO of Sierra Roots aspiring to a similar approach in Nevada County. Charles Durrett, the architect of Valley View. Mayor, Leon Garcia. Councilmember, Mark Joseph. Resident, Arvind Nischal. Community Development Director, Brent Cooper.

I deeply appreciate and acknowledge Kathryn McCamant, my co-conspirator in bringing high-functioning neighborhoods to North America. She was an MDA partner-architect, and she interviewed with the City of American Canyon when presenting the Valley View project. It's one thing to win the schematic design competition, but entirely another to convince them that we had the technical experience and acumen to pull it off.

The builder: Midstate Construction; Wesley E. Barry and Kyle Welsh, project managers; most consultants and artisans saw their work on Valley View as an opportunity to be part of the solution. Midstate Construction, for sure, made itself conspicuous as a better-than-the-average builder with their approach. They came with the heart of a contributor. Like the funders themselves, we all felt that Valley View was something that simply needed to be done. The builders stepped up with a better-than-average attention to detail, and in particular, with careful

SAHA management at VVSH.

Construction meetings every other week. Moving us towards the target of on budget, schedule, and quality.

Susan Friedland. CEO, SAHA.

attention to the budget, quality, and schedule. A project like this brings out the best in everyone. MDA is proud to have worked with Midstate Construction on this project as we have on 3 other similarly scaled housing projects over the years.

The civil engineers: Reichers and Spence Associates (RSA+); Because of the slope and therefore the drainage and the 24-building solution, the site took on a bit of an English muffin character. There were simply nooks and crannies everywhere—therefore the civil engineers had to pay close attention and work overtime throughout the entire process.

The landscape architects: Josephine McProud at McProud and Associates Landscape Architecture; Again because of all of the nooks and crannies. It was a workout. Jo made us all look good in the end as she has on many other projects as well.

Thank you to all of the consultants who made Valley View a reality.

The book: I'd like to thank Jinglin Yang for putting her heart and soul into making this book beautiful. Jinglin Yang who wasn't on the cover at first, but in the end was so saddled with real responsibilities, that the cover called her name. English is not her first language, so the challenge took on even greater dimensions. The book would not be done without her.

Jeanne Dickenson, homeless advocate, who made sure that I focused on who I was talking to and was tenaciously re-directing me over and over again back to whom we were speaking. Ellen Fietz Hall who chimed in and to Diane Durrett and Mike van Mantgem who made sure that people would enjoy reading this story, and to ORO Editions who are just as motivated as we are to get the word out there, "This is doable."

The oh-so-cool crew of McCamant & Durrett Architects.

Early town-wide design input.

The grand opening at Valley View.

Appendix A
Affordable Villages Elsewhere

Affordable tiny houses have been built all across the United States when sizable subsidies could not be found. At times, they are made with volunteer labor, donated materials, donated land, and the contributions of a lot of gifted, dedicated, and motivated professionals and volunteers.

The best one that we know of is Opportunity Village in Eugene, Oregon, where the 30 tiny houses cost on average $8,000 each to build. And where the police have not been called once in six years. The city council voted 8:1 to lease this site yearly in 2013. They have voted 9:0 to continue the lease every year since then. Originally, water was trucked in, and sewage was trucked out. Since then the residents with the help of volunteers added city sewer, city water, solar power and heating to the tiny houses that were built with the residents and volunteer labor. These villages are being built around the U.S. Resident participation is the key to keeping the villages inexpensive places to live. The rent at Opportunity Village, for example, is $30 per month. Affordability was also crucial at a project that MDA designed for Mercy Housing for single mothers and their children in Morgan Hill, California, and also at a five-story project in Oakland for Catholic Charities and at a five-story homeless project in San Francisco.

Eugene Opportunity Village

Appendix B

Picturing the Homeless in California

Percent of the nation's homeless who are veterans: **25%**

Proportion of homeless veterans living in California: **24%**

Percent of the country's overall homeless population who live in California: **20%**

Percentage of recent calls to Nevada County 211 related to homelessness-issues: **24%**

About **1/2** of the land fires in Nevada County in the last 20 years have been started by homeless individuals. Sympathetic citizens say that they have to cook their beans somewhere. Unsympathetic citizens argue that's all the reason we need to move them along.

49er Fire in Nevada County (homeless-started) caused the loss of: **44 homes & 219 structures**

In addition, it burned: **33,000 acres**, with a value of: **$28 million**

Overall cost to suppress the fire: **$7.5 million**

EXHIBIT 1.5: **Estimates of Homeless People**
By State, 2014

Appendix C
The FEMA Emergency Criteria
The emergency before us: Humans are at risk in our community.

FEMA considers homelessness an emergency.

Whether from a hurricane, a wildfire, or the experience of homelessness, they all put ***human lives at RISK***. People without a roof over their heads or the typical support system are at risk, and the longer they remain in this state, the more at risk they become.

For people left out in the cold, whether for a day, a month, a year, or longer experience constant disaster much of it life-threatening. Since homelessness is often chronic for an individual or family, some members of our community live with life-threatening disasters day in and day out.

The emergency before us: Humans are at risk in our community. It is a community emergency.

While people experiencing homelessness do not garner adequate public attention, their impact on other members of the community often does. Fires, unsightly litter and loitering, under-considered hospital visits, and police calls are just some of these ill effects. Numerous wildfires, including one of the largest in the area, have been started by homelessness. The simpliest solution is the community provides a supportive place for them to live.

The emergency before us: Humans are at risk in our community. It is an allocation of resources emergency.

Every day lives and property are put at risk because of homelessness. It is not only imperative that we address this crisis. We can do so with local resources, community willpower, and collective ingenuity.
The emergency before us: Humans are at risk in our community. It is a business emergency.

Business continuity is threatened by local homelessness. Study after study in city after city details a cost to the local government and state. National government expenditures to homeless people are $20,000 to $40,000 less per person than if they are left in the woods.

The emergency before us: Humans are at risk in our community. It is a fiscal responsibility to solve this emergency. The current pandemic exacerbates this condition.

When people experiencing homelessness are provided with a safe, supportive place, local agencies save crucial resources. The savings from a proactive approach to homelessness would provide ample resources to other pressing county issues. From an increased tax burden point of view alone, it is a long-term malfeasance to not proactively address this issue.

The county's overall approach to address the homelessness of some of its residents needs to be multifaceted. It is clear that those strategies that provide housing are most effective and doing so in one place like a tiny house village is the low-hanging fruit (both cost effective and humane).

The emergency before us: Humans are at risk in our community. It is an emergency we must address now.

If immediate action is not taken to reduce the suffering of individuals, families, and our community as a whole, this state of emergency will continue to wreak havoc on our brothers and sisters in need. We can not afford to turn a blind eye to this emergency happening among our people, in our community, to our businesses.

When a devastating wildfire hits some part of our county, we don't stand by and let community members suffer on their own. Let's take that same approach when it comes to the homelessness emergency.

Appendix D

Sample Resident Agreement

Opportunity Village is a transitional village that provides a safe and secure place to be for those currently without housing. It is a self-governing community that is based on five basic rules:

1. No violence to yourselves or others
2. No theft
3. No alcohol, illegal drugs, or drug paraphernalia
4. No persistent, disruptive behavior
5. Everyone must contribute to the operation and maintenance of the Village.

I will be a positive member of this community and contribute toward making it a safe, secure, clean and pleasant place to live. Therefore I agree to the following:

• What I do will be based on love and respect for myself and others.

• I will not disrespect others based on ethnicity, religion, gender, sexual orientation, handicap, lifestyle choices, or economic status. We all have the right to expect dignity and opportunity.

• I will help make OVE a place where everyone feels safe and respected. For my own safety as well as the safety of others, I will not carry a weapon or act violently toward others or myself.

• Since stealing is one of the most upsetting things that can happen in our community, I will not steal and will make the members of the Village Council aware of any stealing I see. I will respect other people's property and community property and I expect other people to respect mine.

• I know that illegal drugs and alcohol use can damage my community. I agree not to use illegal drugs or alcohol while residing in the Village.

- I will honor quiet hours from 10PM to 7AM so that others and myself can stay healthy and rested. I understand that no personal guests will be allowed during that time.

- I want to live in a clean, litter-free, comfortable space where I can bring friends, family and other guests. Also, I know that many communities such as ours get closed down for "health and safety" reasons. I will keep the area in and around where I live clean and orderly, and not store any personal items outside of my building footprint or allocated storage space. I will help keep the community areas clean and will pick up after myself and my pet, if I have one, and keep my pet leashed at all times. I understand that only a limited number of pets will be allowed in the Village in order to maintain an orderly environment.

- I understand that in order to maintain a secure environment there will be a single point of entrance and exit that will be staffed 24/7, and that security shifts will be shared equally among Village residents.

- I know that it can take a lot of work to keep the Village a safe, clean and pleasant place to live. I agree to work at least 10 hours a week on the operation and maintenance of the Village. This includes serving on security teams, helping with kitchen duties, construction projects, maintenance and clean-up crews, helping plan activities and other jobs that need to be shared by community members.

- I also know that there are financial costs to keep the Village running. I will support the goal of self-sufficiency by contributing each month either financially or through sweat equity by participating in micro-business opportunities or fundraising events.

- I will attend the weekly Village meetings, unless I have an acceptable reason for absence, in which case I will find out what went on by reading the meeting notes. I understand that decisions will be made through a majority vote, and that the Board of Directors of the non-profit reserves the right to override decisions made. I agree to abide by all decisions made.

- I affirm that I have completed the Background Check Form honestly along with all other application documents. I understand that if the background check reveals otherwise, I could be asked to leave immediately.

I promise to keep all of these agreements, as well as others that are approved at Village meetings. If I violate any agreements, the members of the Village Council are authorized to ask me to leave temporarily, or, in serious or repeat cases, to leave permanently. I will do so peacefully and not return unless I am authorized to do so.

I know that Opportunity Village is a place where people value community and support each other. I will try to think of ways to make our community a better place to be. When I am concerned or upset with situations in the Village, I will bring these problems to the attention of the appropriate people so that we can work together to figure things out.

Signature: _____

Date: _____

Appendix E

Benefits of an Opportunity Village in Eugene, Oregon and to any Americans Experiencing People Without a Roof in Their Town.

1. Reduces stress on county's emergency resources, such as those responding to calls from homeless persons in outlying areas
2. Bolsters a human resource, offering additional employment potential as village residents-now with a roof over their head-have increased opportunity to hone useful job-related skills
3. Decrease in county finances devoted to short-term housing fixes
4. Promotes compassionate action
5. Upholds principles near-and-dear to spiritual teachings
6. Creates potential to unveil unseen talents of an unacknowledged population
7. Places a face on the issue locally
8. Includes a disenfranchised aspect of the population in a community solution
9. Develops a more wholesome community
10. Reduces litter, as residents will have an established site to store their belongings
11. Minimized strain on cleaning up temporary storage sites of the homeless
12. Reduces potential fire threats from scattered camps in the woods
13. Integrates simple living standards into greater community
14. Acts as a progressive solution
15. Provides a model for other cities, both in California and beyond
16. A highly successful model has been established through Opportunity Village Eugene and similar projects. The precedent has been set for real change
17. This issue is already in the spotlight and this project offers opportunities for demonstrating progress locally
18. Aids in dispelling preconceived notions about this population
19. Offers a social demonstration of communal living
20. Collaboration with existing, respected local non-profits motivated to address homelessness

Appendix F
Faces of Change: Formally Homeless

Photo by Dee Anne Dinelli.

Photo by Dee Anne Dinelli.

Photo by Dee Anne Dinelli.

Photo by Dee Anne Dinelli.

About the Author

Charles Durrett is an architect, author, and advocate of affordable, socially responsible and sustainable design, and who has made major contributions to community-based architecture and cohousing. Charles has designed over fifty cohousing communities in North America and has consulted on many more around the world, having designed an equal number of affordable housing projects. He is the principle architect at McCamant & Durrett Architects, based in Nevada City, California. His work has been featured in Time magazine, New York Times, LA Times, San Francisco Chronicle, The Boston Globe, The Washington Post, The Guardian, Architecture, Architectural Record, Wall Street Journal, The Economist, and a wide variety of other publications.

Along with receiving numerous awards for his contribution to cohousing and community-based architecture, he has given many public presentations, such as two to the U.S. Congress, The Commonwealth Club of California, scores of universities, city councils, and planning commissions around the country. Most important, he continues to devote his time to new cohousing groups and affordable housing developments that are just getting started.

His other books include Creating Cohousing: Building Sustainable Communities, coauthored with Kathryn McCamant, the book that introduced cohousing to the United States. The Senior Cohousing Handbook: A Community Approach to Independent Living, as well as a half-dozen other books about housing. He lives in a 34-unit project, Nevada City Cohousing, in Northern California, a community he designed in which 21 seniors also reside. He previously lived in Doyle Street Cohousing in Emeryville, California, with his family for 12 years. The Oxford English Dictionary credits him, along with partner Kathryn McCamant, with coining the word cohousing.

He realized long ago that developing healthy environments requires starting with the culture—and seeing the much wider array of issues other than the sticks and bricks.

Book Layout and Main Book Organizer

Jinglin Yang, LEED AP, is a designer who grew up in Hunan, China, and also lives in Nevada City Cohousing in Northern California. She is a graduate of Georgia Institute of Technology and earned her master's degree in High Performance Building. She is, as well, a graduate of the University of Oregon, with a Bachelor of Architecture degree. She works for McCamant & Durrett Architects in Nevada City, California. Her focus is on sustainable design, building performance, community-based architecture, and communicating these efforts so that they can be replicated.

Jinglin brought structure and drive to this venture and that's why it got done.

Afterword

If there are some key aspects of this story that you believe needs to be told better so that you can implement a community of this caliber in your town, please do let us know. Also, should you still need to know where to start or have any questions whatsoever about where and how to start to implement a place in your town where people are accommodated, please email me at charles. durrett@cohousingco.com. Or call at 916.716.6721. We know how hard it is, and how straight forward it can be.

The first steps involve locating a site and then obtaining a feasibility investigation; together they usually take a few months. The first step is getting started.

When you are ready to get the ball rolling toward a solution, give us a call. We can help you find a site in your town and do the feasibility study. We offer a seasoned, disciplined approach, designed to bring it to fruition.

Thanks again,
Charles Durrett

Feasibility for New Sites

Determining the feasibility of the site is critical for creating a 21st-century village such as Valley View. There are about 30-50 truly big issues to consider which our firm provides for every project that we undertake. Here are many of them:

1. Attainability, or in the case of sites through government agencies, ability to lease
2. Neighborhood Politics
3. Feasibility Studies (sketches, etc.)
4. Access to Public Transportation
5. Funding
6. Accessible to Services, like groceries, dining, and the like.
7. Toxins
8. Noise
9. Zoning
10. Soils
11. Water/Wetlands
12. Site Analysis (existing buildings; landscape; terrain; flora; fauna)
13. Master Planning
14. Programming (what's the vision and the design criteria)
15. Land Use/Zoning Codes
16. Rezoning
17. Planned Unit Development
18. ADA analysis

Then comes the next steps:

1. Schematic Design/ Building Design
2. Design Development
3. Construction Documentation
4. Construction Budgeting/ Cost Estimating (on going)
5. Interior Design
6. Construction Contracts
7. Construction Administration
8. City Approvals
9. Energy Efficient Design (constant integration at every step)
10. Community Involvement; Support and more.

We often do a few feasibility sketches for any given site, often with the client sitting right there so we can share and develop all necessary assumptions: to determine how many units will fit, parking, outdoor opportunities, what's best for the streetscape (and therefore the town), courtyards, porches, balconies, etc. Please do not hesitate to call us – we can walk you through the unique aspects of your solutions.

Bibliography

McCamant, Kathryn, and Charles Durrett. *Creating Cohousing: Building Sustainable Communities.* New Society Publishers, 2011.

Durrett, Charles. *Revitalizing Our Small Towns: Recent Examples from Southern France.* Habitat Press, 2012.

Durrett, Charles. *The Senior Cohousing Handbook: A Community Approach to Independent Living, 2nd ed.* New Society Publishers, 2009.

Heben, Andrew. *Tent City Urbanism: From Self-Organized Camps to Tiny House Villages.* The Village Collaborative, 2014.

Levitt, Alexandria, and Charles Durrett. *State-Of-The-Art Cohousing: Lessons Learned from Quimper Village.* Kindle Direct Publishing, 2020.

Steinbeck, John. *The Harvest Gypsies: On the Road to the Grapes of Wrath.* Heyday Books, 1988.